D1649112

RAINFOREST CREATURES

RAINFOREST CREATURES

Benita Sen

PowerKiDS
press.

New York

Published in 2008 by The Rosen Publishing Group, Inc.
29 East 21st Street, New York, NY 10010

First Published: 2006
Designed by Q2A Media

Picture Credits:

t: Top, b:Bottom, c: Center
6t: Joy Stein, 6b: Dagmar Schneider, Mindy w.m. Chung, Peter Igel, Keir Davis, 7t: Alle, 7b: Crotalus258,
8b: Carsten Reisinger, 9t: Geckophoto, 9bl: Steffen Foerster Photography, 9br: John Arnold,
10t: Frank Kebschull, 10b: Szombe, 11t: Kathryn Bell, 11b: Javarman, 12t: Amiro, 12b: Luis César Tejo,
13t: Gert Johannes Jacobus Very, 13bl: Johan Swanepoel, 13br: Photomediacom, 15b: Frank Wouters,
16b: Bartholomew Plucinski, 18t: Ryszard | Dreamstime.com, 18-19c: Darko Draskovic, 19t: Cwinegarden,
19b: Martine Oger, 21t: LeonD, 22t: Christophe Namur, 22b: M. Robbemont, 23t: Robert Cumming,
23b: Matthew Gough, 24t: Timothy E. Goodwin, 24b: Julie Fine, 25t: Cathy Jo Simpson, 25b: Ferenc Cegledi, 26t: Xavier Marchant,
26-27b: Vera Bogaerts, 27tl: Vladimir Pomortzeff, 27tr: Hadi Djunaedi, 28t: Outlook,
28b: Michael Lynch, 29t: JeanKern, 29b: Jaana Piira, 30t: Impalastock, 31t: Gregory James Van Raalte,
31b: Grigory Kubatyan, 32t: Fleyeing | Dreamstime.com, 32b: Jerry Dupree, 33t: Martin Plsek,
33b: Joel Bauchat Grant, 34t: Carsten Reisinger, 34b: Holger Wulschlaeger, 35t: Cheryl Kunde,
35b: A&O Maksymenko, 36t: Tony Horton., 36m: Melanie J. Cook, 36b: Radu Razvan,
37t: Michael Pettigrew, 37b: Mike Von Bergen, 38t: Foong Kok Leong, 38b: Sim Kay Seng,
39t: Shamshahrin Shamsudin, 39b: Barbara Brands, 40t: Rainforest Australia, 41t: Cratervalley Photo,
41b: Kirk Peart Professional Imaging, 42t: Steffen Foerster Photography,
43t: Linda Armstrong, 43b: Ra'id Khalil.

Library of Congress Cataloging-in-Publication Data

Sen, Benita.
   Rainforest creatures / Benita Sen.
      p. cm. — (Wild creatures)
   Includes index.
   ISBN-13: 978-1-4042-3893-0 (library binding)
   ISBN-10: 1-4042-3893-X (library binding)
   1. Rain forest animals—Juvenile literature. I. Title.
   QL112.S46 2007
   591.734—dc22

                                          2007008671

Manufactured in China

CONTENTS

LIFE IN THE RAINFOREST

Rainforests, as their name suggests, get a lot of rain. This helps forests to grow. Rainforests are home to millions of plants and animals.

Different strata

There are distinct levels in the rainforest. Each level houses a large variety of animals. The emergent layer is made up of the tops of the tallest trees. The canopy is an umbrella of leaves. Both are home to insects, birds, reptiles, mammals and a few amphibians. The understory is the still, dark area between the floor and the canopy, home to butterflies and birds. A huge variety of creatures live on the forest floor.

The decayed leaves and animal matter provide nutrients, retain water and replenish the soil.

Thanks to the rainforest

Rainforests have a layer of soil that is only 3-4 inches (7.8-10 cm) thick. This soil is rich with decaying leaves and dead animal matter. Tropical rainforests cover seven percent of Earth. The trees absorb carbon dioxide and produce large amounts of oxygen, which people need to breathe. The trees also produce food like nuts, bananas, nutmeg, coffee and tea, as well as useful materials such as rubber. We get medicines from plants like periwinkle and cinchona.

The rainforest is rich with many sources of food and medicine.

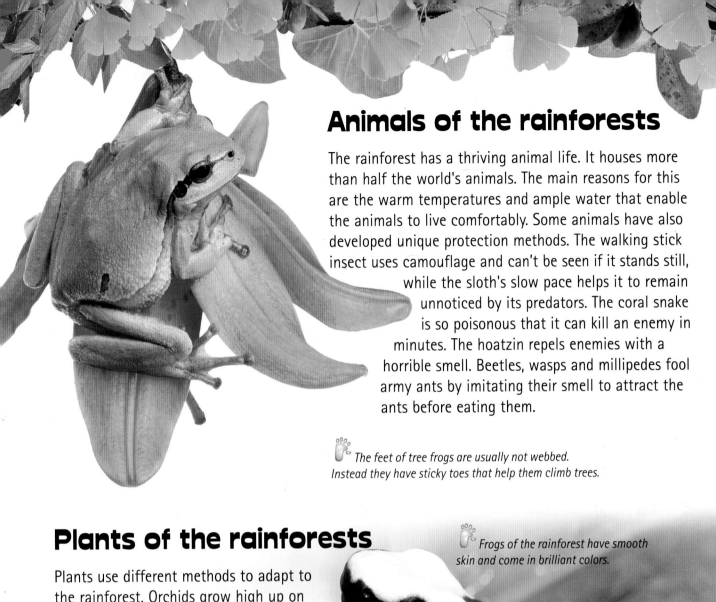

Animals of the rainforests

The rainforest has a thriving animal life. It houses more than half the world's animals. The main reasons for this are the warm temperatures and ample water that enable the animals to live comfortably. Some animals have also developed unique protection methods. The walking stick insect uses camouflage and can't be seen if it stands still, while the sloth's slow pace helps it to remain unnoticed by its predators. The coral snake is so poisonous that it can kill an enemy in minutes. The hoatzin repels enemies with a horrible smell. Beetles, wasps and millipedes fool army ants by imitating their smell to attract the ants before eating them.

The feet of tree frogs are usually not webbed. Instead they have sticky toes that help them climb trees.

Plants of the rainforests

Frogs of the rainforest have smooth skin and come in brilliant colors.

Plants use different methods to adapt to the rainforest. Orchids grow high up on trees and have aerial roots that soak in moisture from the air. Ferns grow on trees. Lianas or climbers send down aerial roots that help younger climbers. Plants need light to survive. The rainforest canopy cuts out most of the sunlight, so rainforest trees have to grow fast to get light. That is why they are tall and slender. Some of these trees, like mangroves, balance with prop roots that grow from the stem and support the tree. Huge leaves also help absorb as much sunlight as possible. Some trees have leaf stalk that turn with the movement of the sun to capture maximum sunlight.

AMPHIBIANS

Caecilians, salamanders and frogs are all amphibians of the rainforest. Amphibians breathe through their skin, so they have to keep it moist. Therefore they spend a lot of time in water.

Caecilian

The caecilian looks like an earthworm or an eel, but is neither. It is also known as rubber eel and Sicilian worm. The caecilian burrows in the moist soil of the rainforest. This vertebrate has jaws and two rows of teeth. Almost blind, it feels its way with its tentacles. The caecilian is 5–14 inches (12.7-35.5 cm) long and about 0.25–1 inch (0.6-2.5 cm) wide. It feeds on insects and worms. Its enemies are birds, fish and snakes.

Salamander

Salamanders have slender bodies, short legs and long tails. They look like lizards but have no scales. Like lizards, these vertebrates are capable of regenerating their lost limbs. Most of them do not have lungs or gills. Salamanders breathe through their moist skin. Most female salamanders lay eggs in water. Salamanders have brightly colored coats and can be poisonous. When teased, some salamanders defend themselves by secreting poisonous liquid from their skins. Salamanders eat insects and worms. Lizards, birds and snakes feed on them.

The limbless caecilian has circular grooves on its body that make it look like an earthworm.

The tiger salamander is mainly terrestrial and usually returns to water only to breed.

Frogs

Rainforests are full of unusual frogs. Frogs are the most common amphibians in a rainforest. Most of these frogs live in trees. Some look like dead leaves, so that they can hide from their enemies. Some, like the red-eyed tree frog of Central America and northern South America, are active at night. Apart from their large, red eyes and red feet, these frogs are bright green with blue sides and yellow stripes. The heart and other organs of the semitransparent glass frog can be seen through its skin!

The red-eyed frog's green coloring helps it to stay hidden among the tree leaves.

CREATURE PROFILE

Common name:	Golden poison-arrow frog
Scientific name:	*Phyllobates terribilis*
Other name:	Poison-dart frog
Found in:	Central and South America
Weight:	About 1 ounce (28 g)
Feed on:	Spiders, insects
Enemies:	Man
Status:	Threatened due to destruction of habitat

Most poison-arrow frogs live on the ground in the leaf litter, hunting tiny insects by the day.

POISON-ARROW FROG

The tiny poison-arrow frog secretes deadly poison from its back. Some people who live in the rainforest tip their arrows with this poison and use them for hunting. These frogs have bright markings on their skin to warn their predators of the danger of feeding on them. The most poisonous is the golden poison-arrow frog of Colombia. A person can die just by licking its back with the tip of his tongue!

The poison of these frogs comes from eating poisonous insects.

LIZARDS

The male basilisk has two crests. One is on its head, the other is on its back.

The rainforest houses a variety of lizards like geckos, iguanas, water dragons and chameleons. These reptiles have unique adaptation techniques that help them survive comfortably in their habitat.

Basilisk

Remember the giant snake that Harry Potter kills? The crested basilisk of the rainforest is named after the same mythical monster that is believed to kill people with a glance! The rainforest basilisk is quite harmless. It is a good climber. Male basiliks have two crests on their body. Females have one. They can run across water, balancing with their long whiplike tail. Their weblike scaled toes help them tread water. Basilisks are 2-2.5 feet (0.6-0.8 m) long. They eat insects, spiders and worms. They, in turn, are food for snakes and large birds.

CHLAMYDOSAURUS

The chlamydosaurus is also known as the frilled lizard. It lives on trees in northern Australia and New Guinea. It has folds of skin around its head. When in danger, the frilled lizard opens the folds to spread its huge frill, 7-14 inches (18-34 cm) wide, to scare away its enemies. The chlamydosaurus, over 7.8 inches (20 cm) long, run on all four limbs. When frightened, they scuttle away on their hind legs. This is why they are also called bicycle lizards. They eat insects and smaller lizards.

Apart from helping to scare predators, the opened frill also helps the lizard to regulate its body temperature.

Gecko

Geckos are the only lizards that can make sounds. They are comfortable hunting at night since they have good eyesight. Geckos eat insects and sometimes even their own eggs. Snakes are the gecko's biggest enemy. The northern leaf-tailed gecko has a large tail that looks like a leaf. Geckos are between 6 and 14 inches (15-35 cm) long.

The gecko family includes over 700 species!

KOMODO DRAGON

The fierce Komodo dragons are the world's biggest lizards. Komodos live in Indonesia and get their name from Komodo Island. They have strong jaws, a forked tongue and sharp claws. Active during the day, they are good runners, climbers and swimmers. They hunt all kinds of animals and sometimes even attack people. They also feed on dead animals. Komodo bites can kill because their mouth is full of deadly bacteria that poison their victim's blood.

CREATURE PROFILE

Common name:	Komodo dragon
Scientific name:	*Varanus komodoensis*
Found in:	Indonesia
Weight:	About 300 pounds (135 kg)
Length:	9 feet (2.8 m)
Feed on:	Other lizards, deer, goats, wild boar and dead animals
Status:	Threatened due to habitat destruction and hunting

The komodo dragon is quite agile and athletic and can run at a speed of about 11 miles per hour (18 km/h).

CAIMANS AND CROCODILES

Caimans, alligators and crocodiles belong to the crocodilian family. These large, semiaquatic reptiles are found in rainforests.

Caimans

Caimans resemble alligators but are smaller and thicker. Their length ranges from 5 to 9 feet (1.5-2.7 m). There are about six sub species of caimans. The spectacled caimans are the most common. Because of their modest size they are widely used in pet trade along with dwarf caimans. The largest are the black caimans that can grow up to 20 feet (6 m) in length. These dangerous monsters are mainly found in the Amazon Basin.

The caiman's webbed feet and long tail help it to swim and steer well in water.

Alligators

The eyes of all crocodilians are located on top of their heads, enabling them to see even when they are in water.

Most alligators are native to the rainforests in America, with the exception of the Chinese alligator. Alligators are excellent hunters. Their powerful vision and hearing, together with their agility helps them catch aquatic and terrestrial animals with ease. They are known to make "gator holes," or pools of water, during the dry season.

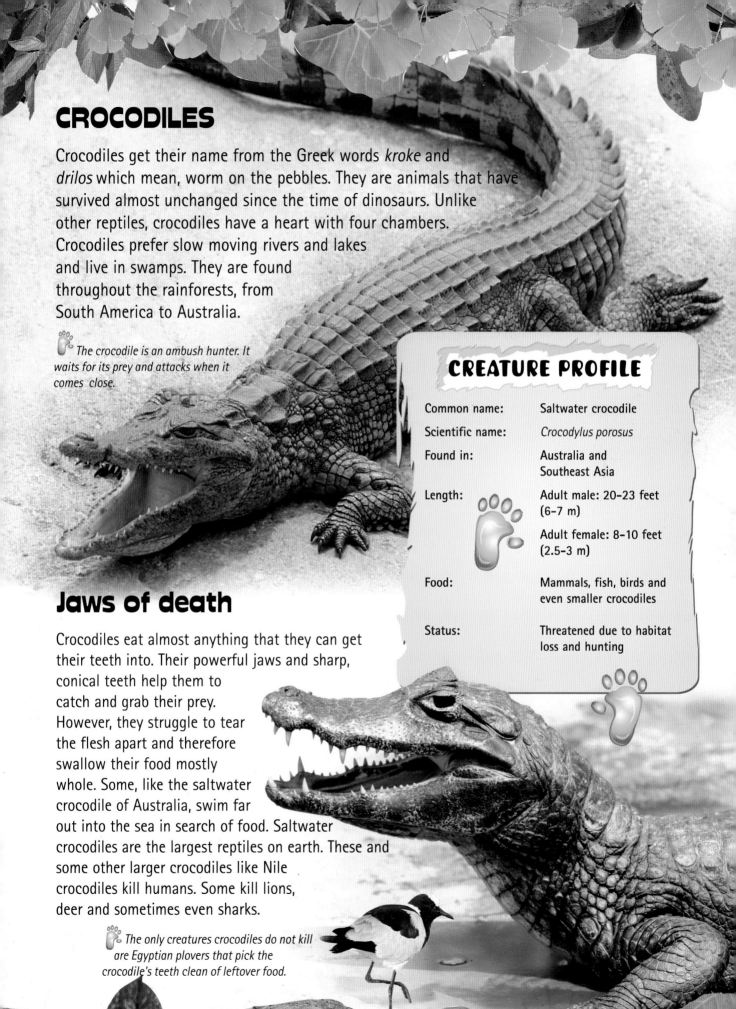

CROCODILES

Crocodiles get their name from the Greek words *kroke* and *drilos* which mean, worm on the pebbles. They are animals that have survived almost unchanged since the time of dinosaurs. Unlike other reptiles, crocodiles have a heart with four chambers. Crocodiles prefer slow moving rivers and lakes and live in swamps. They are found throughout the rainforests, from South America to Australia.

The crocodile is an ambush hunter. It waits for its prey and attacks when it comes close.

Jaws of death

Crocodiles eat almost anything that they can get their teeth into. Their powerful jaws and sharp, conical teeth help them to catch and grab their prey. However, they struggle to tear the flesh apart and therefore swallow their food mostly whole. Some, like the saltwater crocodile of Australia, swim far out into the sea in search of food. Saltwater crocodiles are the largest reptiles on earth. These and some other larger crocodiles like Nile crocodiles kill humans. Some kill lions, deer and sometimes even sharks.

The only creatures crocodiles do not kill are Egyptian plovers that pick the crocodile's teeth clean of leftover food.

CREATURE PROFILE

Common name:	Saltwater crocodile
Scientific name:	*Crocodylus porosus*
Found in:	Australia and Southeast Asia
Length:	Adult male: 20-23 feet (6-7 m)
	Adult female: 8-10 feet (2.5-3 m)
Food:	Mammals, fish, birds and even smaller crocodiles
Status:	Threatened due to habitat loss and hunting

BOAS

Boas are large, nonvenomous snakes usually found in the rainforests of South America and Central America. There are about 30 species of boas, of which the boa constrictor and anaconda are the best-known.

Squeezing the life out

The boa is not poisonous. It kills its prey using a unique method known as constriction. The boa waits for its prey to come near or approaches it silently. It grabs the prey and wraps its body around it. The boa tightens its coils around its struggling prey, until it is unable to breathe and dies. The boa then swallows this dead victim.

After choking its prey, the boa opens its huge mouth and swallows it, head first.

BOA CONSTRICTOR

One of the better-known species of boas, the boa constrictor is found in various habitats ranging from arid deserts to wet tropical rainforests. It, however, prefers dry land or trees, and is not found near water. The boa constrictor is the second largest snake in the boa family. It can grow to a maximum length of 18 feet (5.5 m). This snake feeds on large lizards, birds, rodents and small mammals. The boa constrictor is particularly fond of bats. The snake usually hangs from tree branches to grab bats that fly past. It then suffocates the prey and swallows it.

The emerald tree boa is native to South America. Its green skin helps it to blend into the rainforest vegetation.

A giant among snakes

There are four species of anacondas. Of these, the green anaconda is the best known. It is not only the largest of all boas, but is also the heaviest snake in the world. This gigantic snake is usually 20 feet (6 m) long and weighs about 500 pounds (250 kg). Some green anacondas are believed to grow over 32 feet (10 m) in length and weigh more than 1,000 pounds (500 kg)! This snake's skin is olive green in color, with oval black spots along its body and two long stripes on its head.

The color and pattern of the green anaconda helps it blend into its habitat.

An aquatic life

Anacondas are the only boas that prefer living in water to living on land. These snakes are therefore also known as water boas. Anacondas are usually found in slow-moving streams or swamps. During the day, they lie in shallow water or bask in the sun on low branches overhanging streams or swamps. Like all boas, anacondas are nocturnal and hunt mainly at night. They lie submerged with only their eyes and nose above the water. When prey comes by, the anacondas grab it with their powerful jaws and drag it underwater to drown it.

The anaconda's nostrils and eyes are on the top of its head allowing it to see and breathe even when its body is submerged.

CREATURE PROFILE

Common name:	Green anaconda
Scientific name:	*Eunectes murinus*
Found in:	The Amazon and Orinoco basins, and the Guianas in South America
Weight:	Adult males: up to 297 pounds (135 kg)
	Adult females: up to 551 pounds (250 kg)
Length:	Adult males: 12–16 feet (3.7–4.8 m)
	Adult females: 20–26 feet (6–8 m)
Prey:	Fish, snakes, amphibians, rodents, medium-sized mammals like deer and caiman
Enemies:	Humans. People kill anacondas out of fear.
Status:	Protected from illegal pet trade and hunting. The number of anacondas in the wild is unknown.

PYTHONS

Pythons are nonpoisonous snakes found in Africa, Asia, the Pacific islands and Australia. There are about 25 species of pythons.

Largest in the world

Pythons grow for as long as they live. They range from 3 to 33 feet (1-10 m) and weigh up to 300 pounds (140 kg). The reticulated python is the longest snake in the world. One was measured at 32.9 feet (10 m). Pythons pin their prey down with their teeth, and then coil themselves around it. Like boas, they squeeze the prey tightly until it suffocates. Then, they swallow it, head-first. Pythons eat monkeys, deer, goats and other smaller animals.

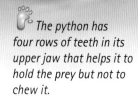 The python has four rows of teeth in its upper jaw that helps it to hold the prey but not to chew it.

Elastic jaws

The python's upper and lower jaws are attached with ligaments, or bands that expand like elastic. This allows it to open its mouth wide and swallow the prey whole. The acid juices in the python's stomach digest the food. Depending on the size of the prey, the python may take over several days, or even weeks to digest it. Therefore, a python can go a long time between meals. A python that has just eaten can barely move and is often attacked by its enemies at this time.

 The stretchy bands that join the python's upper and lower jaws allow it to swallow prey wider than its head.

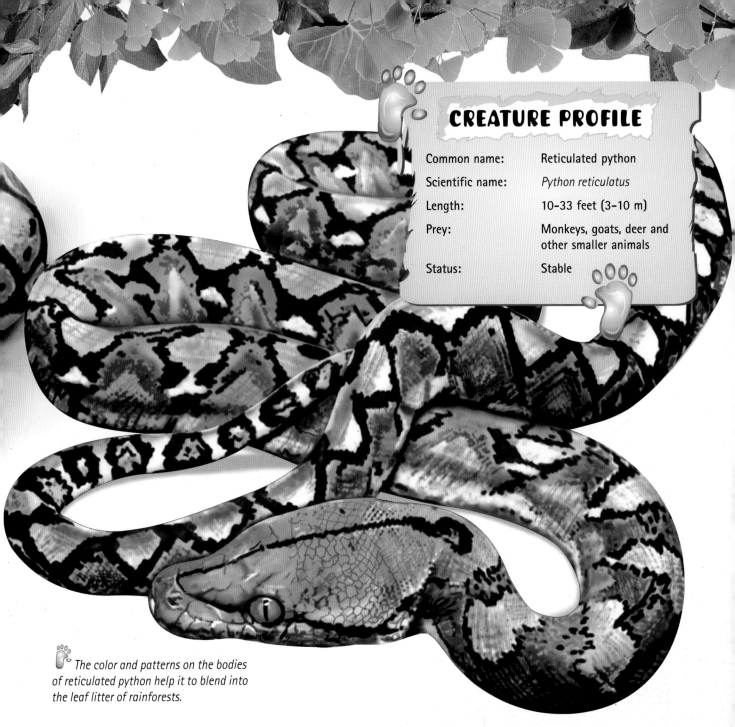

CREATURE PROFILE

Common name:	Reticulated python
Scientific name:	*Python reticulatus*
Length:	10–33 feet (3–10 m)
Prey:	Monkeys, goats, deer and other smaller animals
Status:	Stable

The color and patterns on the bodies of reticulated python help it to blend into the leaf litter of rainforests.

Snakes with feet?

Pythons have scaly, dry skin. Most pythons have lips that can sense their prey. Unlike boa constrictors, pythons have teeth at the front and center of their upper jaw. Snakes are believed to have evolved from lizardlike creatures. Over the years, they lost their legs. However, pythons have two tiny claws at the back, where the hind legs may have been. These claws are longer in male pythons. Pythons, unlike most other snakes, have two lungs.

A nest for eggs

A female python lays 15 to 100 eggs. She arranges them in a pile and coils herself around the eggs until they hatch. Most pythons prefer to stay on the ground, hiding among the underbrush. Pythons are good climbers. Some, like the green tree python, live only in trees. Pythons are also able swimmers. Sometimes, pythons hide in streams with their heads above water, waiting for birds or small mammals to come to the water's edge.

RODENTS

Rodents are mammals with two incisors, or front teeth, on the upper jaw and two on the lower. They get their name from the Latin *rodere* (gnaw) and *dentis* (teeth). Their teeth grow continuously to replace the parts that are worn down from their almost constant gnawing.

Agouti

Agoutis are related to the guinea pig. Agoutis live in Central America, Mexico, and northern South America. They eat plants, fruit, seeds and roots during the day. As they eat, sitting up on their hind legs and holding the food in their front paws, they scatter seeds, which help new trees to grow. Agoutis have blackish-brown fur. Some have tiny tails about 1 inch (2.5 cm) long. They can run fast and swim well. When they are frightened, they freeze on the spot. Agoutis are 16-24 inches (41-61 cm) long and weigh about 8.8 pounds (4 kg). Agoutis are eaten by eagles, snakes, ocelots and jaguars.

Agoutis feed on fruit and other parts of plants.

COYPU

This rodent has bright orange colored front teeth. The coypu is most active at dusk or at dawn. About 15-24 inches (40–60 cm) long and weighing between 10 and 20 pounds (5–9 kg), the coypu has reddish-brown fur on top and gray fur below. Its long tail has little hair. Coypus eat plants and grains. Its webbed hind feet makes it a good swimmer, but it is clumsy on land. Wolves and snakes hunt coypus. The coypu is found in Asia, Europe and the Americas.

The coypu is hunted for its soft, velvety underfur.

Capybara

Capybaras are the largest rodent in the world. They are found in Central America and South America. Capybaras live in swamps. These herbivores eat water plants, grass, fruit and grains. The brown furred capybaras are social animals and live in small groups of about six to twenty and talk to each other with barks and whistles. A female capybara gives birth to between one and six babies that are born with fur and can see right away.

CREATURE PROFILE

Common name:	Capybara
Scientific name:	*Hydorchaeris hydrochaeris*
Length:	40-52 inches (102-132 cm)
Weight:	60-100 pounds (27-50 kg)
Status:	Stable

Capybaras can dive and may stay underwater for as long as five minutes.

Enemy!

Capybaras have many enemies like the ocelot, eagle and jaguar, and snakes like the anaconda. Even people eat them. When they sense danger, they let out a warning click, dash into the water and swim to safety. Their webbed feet help them swim well. They enjoy rolling around in the mud.

The capybara uses water for shelter against dangers but rests on dry ground.

OCELOTS AND JAGUARS

Jaguars and ocelots belong to the cat family. They are found in the rainforests of Central America and South America.

OCELOT

The ocelot looks a bit like a pet cat. However, it is a wild cat that has almost disappeared from North America. The ocelot likes to live and hunt alone. It can see well at night, which is when it usually comes out. It rests during the day. It is comfortable living and even sleeping in the lower branches of trees. However, it also hunts on the ground. Ocelots are good swimmers and great climbers.

The ocelot is very agile and a fast climber. It has sharp vision and hearing capacity that help it to hunt efficiently.

Ocelot facts

A female ocelot gives birth to between one and four cubs. The cubs are born with their eyes closed. Ocelots often catch birds, monkeys, snakes, frogs, cattle, poultry and even fish for their meals. Ocelots are about 34-57 inches (85-145 cm) long, including the tail. Their weight is between 22 and 33 pounds (10-15 kg). Their unique coat, with spots and stripes, helps them hide among the trees and the undergrowth.

The color of the ocelot's fur ranges from tawny yellow to light gray depending on its habitat.

JAGUAR

Jaguars are the third largest wild cat, smaller only than the tiger and the lion. Jaguars are heavier than leopards and have a stockier build. They are the most powerful cats in the Americas. Their tawny yellow fur has rosettes with spots inside. Jaguars have large heads and short, sturdy legs. Their muscled forelegs help them to drag prey more than six times their body weight.

REGION PROFILE

Common name:	Jaguar
Scientific name:	*Panthera onca*
Length:	5.3–6 feet (1.62–1.83 m) excluding tail
Length of tail:	18–30 inches (45–75 cm)
Height at shoulder:	27–30 inches (67–76 cm)
Weight:	124–333 pounds (56–151 kg)
Prey:	Deer, caiman, frogs, fish, cattle, mice, birds, tapir
Status:	Endangered due to hunting and habitat destruction

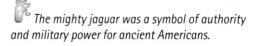 The mighty jaguar was a symbol of authority and military power for ancient Americans.

Powerful hunter

Jaguars can climb trees and swim well. This helps them to hunt a wide variety of prey. They are also fast runners. However, they don't like to give their prey a long chase. They prefer to stalk and then pounce. Jaguars feed on a wide range of animals, from deer to mice. Jaguars have a unique way of killing their prey. Unlike many other hunting animals, which bite the spine of their prey, jaguars puncture their prey's skull. This can sometimes cause them to break a tooth. Jaguars eat 10–70 pounds (5–32 kg) of flesh every day.

The female jaguar gives birth to between one and four cubs and trains them to hunt for two years.

TIGERS

The tiger is one of the animals at the top of the food chain. Tigers help maintain the balance of nature by feeding on animals that eat plants. If tigers did not eat these animals, they would eat up too many plants.

Tigers

Tigers are found in Asia. They are members of the cat family. Like other cats, they see well at night. They have claws that can be drawn back into their paws. The tiger's canine teeth are the largest among land carnivores. Tigers live alone, except when they have cubs. They mark out their territory with scratch marks on trees and with urine.

The tiger is a good swimmer and often likes to cool off in shallow water.

Food for a king

Tigers eat animals like deer, wild boar, rabbits and cattle. When food sources are scarce, they will even eat fish and frogs. Once they spot prey, they follow it stealthily. Their padded paws make sure that they move silently. After a short run, they pounce on the prey and bite its neck. One in every 20 chases ends in a kill. Tigers can eat 40 pounds (18 kg) at a time. They can live without food for several days. A female tiger gives birth to two to four cubs, which she nurses for about six months. The cubs learn to kill their own food within 18 months.

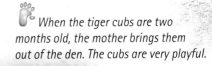

When the tiger cubs are two months old, the mother brings them out of the den. The cubs are very playful.

ROYAL BENGAL TIGER

The Royal Bengal tiger gets its name from the mangrove forests of the Sunderbans in India, where many of them live. They are also found in parts of India and Myanmar. Bengal tigers have orange fur with long vertical stripes in brown, gray or black that help them hide in the tall grass.

The Royal Bengal tiger is the national animal of India.

CREATURE PROFILE

Common name:	Bengal tiger
Scientific name:	*Panthera tigris*
Length without tail:	4.5-9 feet (1.37-2.7 m)
Tail:	3-4 feet (0.9-1.2 m)
Weight:	Male 397-569 pounds (180-258 kg)
	Female: 220-353 pounds (100-160 kg)
Status:	Critically endangered due to habitat loss and hunting.

SUMATRAN TIGER

The Sumatran tiger is found on the island of Sumatra in Indonesia. It is the smallest of all tigers. There are only about 500 Sumatran tigers left. These tigers can move faster than other tigers and have narrower stripes than the Royal Bengal tiger.

Every tiger has unique stripes, like human fingerprints. Sumatran tigers have the most stripes of all tiger species.

GORILLAS AND CHIMPANZEES

Gorillas and chimpanzees eat fruit and help to scatter the seeds. This ensures new trees grow through the forest.

Chimpanzee

Chimpanzees are animals closely related to humans. There are two species of chimpanzees, the common chimpanzee and the bonobo or pygmy chimpanzee. Chimpanzees are tailless. They belong to the order of primates and are intelligent beings. Their brain is half as large as ours. Like humans, they can solve problems by using tools. They dig insects out of holes using sticks and make tools from grass stems, bark and leaves. They eat about 200 different kinds of food, including fruit, leaves, honey, ants and small birds.

The opposable thumbs and toes of chimpanzees help them grasp objects.

Chimpanzees are good climbers and can swing from tree to tree.

Among the leaves

Chimpanzees sleep at night in nests that they build among the branches of trees. When on the ground, they walk on all fours. The arms of the common chimp are more than half its height. The shorter bonobo's arms are even longer. Mother chimpanzees have one child at a time. Chimpanzees make more than 34 different calls. Most of what we know about chimpanzees is thanks to Jane Goodall, who began studying them in Tanzania's Gombe Preserve in July 1960.

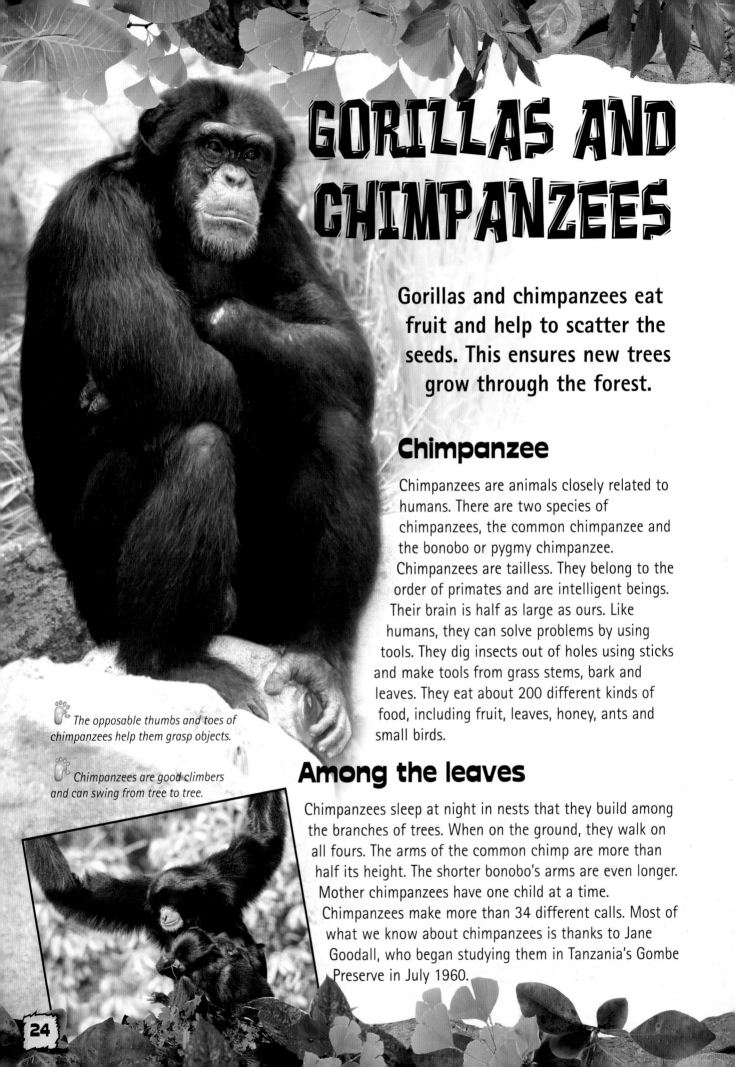

Gorilla

Gorillas are named after a tribe of hairy women called *gorillai* in Greek. They look fierce but are gentle and intelligent. They live in Zaire, Rwanda, Uganda, Nigeria, Gabon, Congo, Cameroon and Central African Republic. Gorillas walk on all four limbs and use the knuckles of their front limbs for support. Gorillas eat leaves, flowers, fungus and even insects.

Each gorilla has a slightly different nose that helps them to recognize each other!

The mother gorilla cares tenderly for her babies who ride on her belly or on her sides until they are about a year old.

CREATURE PROFILE

Common name:	Gorilla
Scientific name:	Western gorilla: *Gorilla gorilla*; eastern gorilla: *Gorilla beringei*
Color:	Black or brownish-gray. Adult males have a silver patch on their back.
Height:	Adult male: about 5.6 feet (1.7 m)
	Adult female: about 5 feet (1.5 m)
Weight:	Adult male: 300–500 pounds (136–227 kg)
	Adult female: 150–250 pounds (68–113 kg)
Status:	Endangered due to habitat loss and hunting

Social animals

Gorillas live in groups consisting of as many as 30 members. Each group has one adult male or silverback, three or four adult females and their children. Female gorillas make caring mothers. Young gorillas spend about four years with their mothers. Both parents defend their children when in danger, even if it costs them their lives. Gorillas talk to each other using about 25 different sounds, from hoots to screams and barks.

The slender and long-limbed gibbon can travel quickly from tree to tree.

OTHER APES

The main difference between apes and monkeys is that apes are tailless. Apes also have better senses of sight and smell.

Gibbon

The gibbon family is rather large. It includes about nine different apes like the siamang of Malaysia and Sumatra, the white-handed lar of Malay and the gray wou-wou of Java. Gibbons are slim and have woolly fur. They have long arms, which they use to swing from trees. They are the only apes that walk on their hind legs. Gibbons make many different sounds to communicate with each other. Gibbons eat fruit, flowers, leaves, birds, insects and eggs.

Loving family

Only six out of every one hundred animal species remain with only one partner. Gibbons are among them. The mother usually gives birth to one baby at a time, and a family of gibbons can include four children of ages up to 10 years old. Sometimes, especially at dawn, the parents break into a song and some of the children join in. The female gibbon, larger than her mate, leads the family. Gibbons do not build nests. When they sleep, they sit with their head tucked into their lap and wrap their arms around their knees.

Gibbons have a whitish gray ring that surrounds their black face.

The orangutan is the only big ape found in Asia.

The mother orangutan nurses her baby for three years.

Orangutan

Orangutan, in the Malay language means, "man of the jungle." The orangutan is an ape from Asia and is found only in Sumatra, in Indonesia, and Borneo. The orangutan has a bulky body and bowlegs. This ape lives in trees most of its life and swings from one branch to another using long, strong arms. It has four fingers and a thumb that is at an angle from the fingers. Its feet have four toes plus a bigger toe that is at an angle, so they can grasp branches with both their hands and their feet. On the ground, they walk on all fours. Every evening, this ape builds a nest on a tree to rest.

A lot to eat

Orangutans eat plants and animals. They love fruits, seeds, young shoots, fresh leaves, flowers and plant bulbs. They also eat insects, eggs, birds and small mammals. Orangutans prefer to live alone. These intelligent animals can use tools to solve problems. Some make cups out of leaves to drink water from. Others use leaves as umbrellas. Male orangutans have a throat pouch that helps them produce loud calls that can be heard over 0.6 miles (1 km) away.

CREATURE PROFILE

Common name:	Orangutan
Scientific name:	*Pongo pygmaeus*
Height:	Adult male: 3.2–4.5 feet (1–1.4 m)
	Adult female: 2.6–3.5 feet (0.8–1.1 m)
Weight:	Adult male: 170–200 pounds (77–90 kg)
	Adult female: 81–110 pounds (37–50 kg)
Enemy:	Humans
Status:	Endangered due to habitat loss. Baby orangutans are also sold as pets.

MONKEYS

Monkeys are important to the health of the rainforests. Most monkeys help to disperse the seeds of trees when they eat the fruit, either by throwing the seeds away or passing them out with their dung.

SAKI MONKEY

Saki monkeys are found north of the Amazon in South America. The male saki monkey has a white face and the female has white markings on its face. Their strong hind legs help them to leap. They eat fruit and seeds and have large canine teeth that help crack open nuts and other food. Saki monkeys also feed on small bats, squirrels and mice. Unlike most other monkeys, these monkeys live in small family groups consisting of the parent monkeys and their young ones.

The spider monkey displays great acrobatic skill while swinging from tree to tree.

SPIDER MONKEY

Spider monkeys are found between southern Brazil and central Mexico. They have long, slim arms and legs that lend them their name. They can take amazingly long leaps. Spider monkeys have the longest and strongest tail of all monkeys. Their tail is prehensile and helps grasp branches well. The tail acts like a fifth limb and lends support when the monkeys swing from tree to tree. While swinging through trees, they suspend their bodies, using their hands to grip one branch at a time. They eat fruit, nuts, seeds, leaves, and insects.

The saki monkey prefers to live in the lower canopy and the understory levels of the rainforests.

WOOLLY MONKEY

The woolly monkey has a large head and a thick body. It gets its name from the thick coat that helps keep the rain off it. The woolly monkey lives among the upper branches of trees and seldom comes down. Its prehensile tail helps it get a good grip and prevents it from falling. It has an opposable toe that helps to grasp well. Its thumb, however, isn't opposable. Woolly monkeys live in groups with membership ranging from 5 to 40. It eats fruit, leaves and insects.

The tail of the woolly monkey helps it to grip branches for support when it climbs and swings through trees.

CREATURE PROFILE

Common name:	Howler monkey
Scientific name:	*Alouatta senioculus*
Height:	2-4 feet (0.6-1.2 m)
Weight:	8-22 pounds (3.5-10 kg)
Diet:	Leaves, fruit, flowers insects
Status:	Endangered

HOWLER MONKEY

The howler monkey lives in southern Brazil, northern Argentina, Paraguay and Bolivia. It is the largest American monkey. It has a large, hollow hyoid, which is the bone supporting the tongue. This helps the monkey to produce and amplify sound. The howler monkey has the loudest roar among all land animals. Their roar can be heard more than 3 miles (4.8 km) away! It lives in the canopy of trees and spends most of its time on the tree, seldom coming down on the forest floor. It is active in the day. It feeds on leaves, fruit, seeds flowers and insects like maggots. The tip of the underside of its tail is worn bare from gripping rough branches.

The male howler monkey is dark brown to black in color, while the female monkey has a lighter shade of brown fur.

SLOTHS

Sloth means laziness. This furry, arboreal (of the trees) mammal of the rainforest canopies of Central America and South America gets its name because of its slow movement.

The sloth's muscles are not well developed for walking upright. It spends most of its time hanging upside-down from trees.

Upside down

Sloths spends most of their lives hanging upside-down from trees. They move, sleep, feed and even give birth while hanging from the trees. The only time they touch the ground is when they move to another tree. That is when their enemies, like jaguars and ocelots, often attack them. Sloths have thick brown fur. Some look green because of the algae on their fur. This helps them hide in the leaves. They lick their algae covered fur for nutrition.

Eat green

Sloths are herbivores or plant-eaters. They prefer to eat fresh and young leaves, but also feed on fruits and shoots. The sloth's stomach has many compartments. This helps them to digest leaves, which can take a sloth almost a month. Some sloths eat insects and small lizards. Since they have no front teeth, they use their hard lips to cut leaves from branches. They eat so much that their small molar teeth get worn down. These teeth keep growing throughout the sloth's life. Sloths do not need to drink water—they get moisture from juicy leaves and dewdrops that they lick.

The sloth holds on to tree branches with strong, hooked claws on its feet.

Good night

Sloths sleep for 15 to 18 hours during the day and are active at night. Male sloths like to live alone, but female sloths sometimes live together. The mother sloth has one baby each year.

CREATURE PROFILE

Common name:	Sloth
Scientific name:	Two-toed sloth: *Choloepus hoffmanni*
	Three-toed sloth: *Bradypus tridactylus*
Lives in:	South America and Central America
Length:	16–29 inches (41–74 cm)
Status:	Some species are endangered.

The sloth curls up while sleeping, placing its head between its arms and legs to blend with the tree.

The sloth's main forms of protection against its enemies are camouflage and its extremely slow movement.

Two toes or three?

Some sloths, like the unau, have two toes. Other species, like the ai, have three. They have two strong claws on their front feet and three on their back feet. These claws give them a good grip. Sloths have big eyes and long legs. Two-toed sloths do not have tails and their front and back legs are almost the same size. In three-toed sloths, the back legs are longer. They have a small tail. These shy creatures are mostly silent, but sometimes sloths let out a cry or a hiss.

OTHER MAMMALS

Rainforests are home to other smaller mammals too. They are usually secretive and nocturnal. This helps them to hide from their predators.

TARSIER

Tarsiers get their name from the long tarsus, or ankle bones, on their feet. They need their goggle-eyes to see while they scuttle around at night. Their long hind legs come in handy when they jump to catch an insect. Tarsiers are a little bigger than rats. Tiny as they are, they are good hunters and eat birds, lizards and snakes. Tarsiers are found in Indonesia, Borneo and the Philippine Islands.

Soft pads on the fingers and toes help tarsiers to grip the branches while climbing.

ECHIDNA

Echidnas, or spiny anteaters, were named after a Greek monster. They are toothless and feed on ants and termites. Their long snout helps them dig out food. Echidnas, like the platypus, are monotremes, or mammals that lay eggs and suckle their young. The female echidna lays one leathery egg and deposits it into a pouch on her stomach. The egg hatches in ten days. The baby, or puggle, lives in the pouch for about 50 days. Echidnas are found in Australia and New Guinea.

The echidna is covered with coarse hair and spines.

KINKAJOU

The kinkajou is an interesting mammal. Belonging to the raccoon family, this small animal has the face of a bear cub, otterlike body and the tail of a monkey! It is sometimes called nightwalker because it comes out at night to eat fruit, flowers, insects, small animals and birds. It is also called honey bear since it enjoys licking honey from hives. During the day, the mammal sleeps on trees, wrapping its prehensile tail, about 15-22 inches (40-56 cm) long, around branches to prevent from falling. The Kinkajou lives on trees in Central America and South America. It moves quickly from tree to tree. When it is startled, it claws and bites its enemies, including the fox, jaguar and ocelot, with its sharp teeth. Its saliva is poisonous.

The kinkajou has a rounded head, small ears and sharp teeth. Its body has soft brown fur.

The platypus swims smoothly using its webbed front paws. On land it moves by gripping the soil with its claws.

CREATURE PROFILE

Common name:	Duck-billed platypus
Scientific name:	*Ornithorhynchus natinus*
Body length:	11.8-18 inches (30-45 cm)
Tail length:	4-6 inches (10-15 cm)
Status:	Stable due to acts that protect it from illegal hunting

DUCK-BILLED PLATYPUS

The duck-billed platypus gets its name from the Greek words, *platys*, meaning broad and *pous*, meaning foot. Its flat snout looks like a duck's bill. It is found in eastern Australia and lives on land and in water. It has brown fur on its body and flat tail that helps to keep it warm. The female platypus lays two to three eggs at a time and suckles its young. The platypus has webbed feet that make it a good swimmer. It eats insects and shrimp. The male platypus has a spur on each hind foot that lets out a strong poison to protect it from enemies.

BUTTERFLIES

Most of the butterflies in the world are found in the rainforests, especially those in South America. Peru alone is home to 6,000 species of butterflies!

JULIA BUTTERFLY

The julia butterfly is a beautiful insect with orange wings outlined in black. It has a wingspan of 3.2-3.6 inches (82-92 mm). Females are lighter in color with more black markings than the males. This butterfly is found from Brazil to southern Texas and Florida and is a strong flier. Some of its favorite nectar is found in the flowers of lantana and shepherd's needle. The female lays her eggs on newly grown leaves. Julia caterpillars eat these leaves once they hatch.

The julia butterfly has a bright orange color and looks stunning against the green rainforest environment!

BLUE MORPHO BUTTERFLY

Blue morpho butterflies live in Brazil, Costa Rica and Venezuela. Their wings are blue on top and brown underneath. When these large butterflies rest, the brown color, spotted with bronze, is visible. Blue morphos drink the juice of rotting fruit. They give off an unpleasant smell when they are disturbed. Their hairy caterpillars are reddish-brown and have light green spots on their back.

The blue morpho is a big butterfly with a wing span of 6 inches (15 cm).

A monarch butterfly drinking nectar from milkweed.

MONARCH BUTTERFLY

Monarchs are the fastest butterfly in the world. They can fly 17 miles (27 km) in an hour. Swarms of monarchs migrate every year from Canada to the rainforests of Central America. Some of them fly over 2,000 miles (3,218 km). These butterflies are poisonous because their larvae feed on poisonous milkweed. This keeps them safe from predators, who become ill and remember never to eat them again. Monarchs drink nectar from milkweed, lantana, lilac, dogbane, red clover and thistle flowers. Monarchs have a wingspan of 3.4-4.7 inches (8.6-12.4 cm).

BLUE MOUNTAIN BUTTERFLY

The blue mountain swallowtail lives in Australia, New Guinea and Indonesia. The male is a brilliant blue and black. The swallowtail gets its name from the two long tails that grow from the tips of its wings. The pupa is green, and so is the caterpillar. These butterflies are so blue, that males often mistake anything blue for a female swallowtail. Birds have a difficult time catching these butterflies, since the bright color distracts them. These butterflies are strong fliers.

CREATURE PROFILE

Common name:	Blue mountain swallowtail
Scientific name:	*Papilio ulysses*
Other names:	Ulysses, blue emperor, and mountain blue butterfly.
Length:	4 inches (11 cm)
Wingspan:	5.5 inches (14 cm)
Status:	Not threatened

The blue mountain butterfly has brilliantly colored wings.

OTHER INSECTS

Insects are creatures that have three pairs of jointed legs, a head, a thorax and abdomen, a hard outer skeleton, a pair of antennae and wings. Some, like the hummingbird flower mite, are so tiny that they can fit inside the nostrils of hummingbirds!

Beetles

There are millions of beetles in the rainforests. Jewel beetles have bright colors on their wings and shine like gems. Most of them feed on nectar while their larvae, or young, get their food by boring into wood. The black male rhinoceros beetle has one horn sticking out in front of its head. The Hercules beetle has a pincer that looks like a stinger, but it is actually only used to scare off enemies.

Here is the rainbow-colored beetle of the rainforest.

Bee

Of all the rainforest creatures that help pollinate flowers, bees are the busiest and most important. Many of them, like the tiny tube bees, do not sting. They sip sweat off humans so are also called sweat bees. Other bees do not bother to gather pollen. Instead, they feed on dead animals. Some bees make their nests from plant resins they collect from the nests of other bees.

The bee sucks nectar from flowers using its proboscis.

Ants

There are more ants than mammals in the rainforest. About three out of every ten creatures in the Amazon basin are ants. They make up 86 percent of the animals found at the canopy level. In Peru, 43 different species of ants were seen on one tree alone. One single colony can house millions of residents. These include the queen ant, the males and an army of female workers who have no wings. The queen ant lays over 100 million eggs in a day!

Ants help to clean the forest floor of dead and dying insects.

CREATURE PROFILE

Common name:	Leafcutter ants
Scientific name:	*Acromyrmex* (24 species); *Atta* (15 species)
Found in :	Central America and South America
Productivity:	Can strip bare one lemon tree in a single day
Enemy:	Phorid fly
Status:	Plentiful

Many ants

The most aggressive type of ants are blind army ants. Honeydew ants feed some of their own young so much honey that the babies turn into food tanks for the adult ants during the dry season. Leafcutter ants cut and carry leaves on their back to their nests. Each leafcutter ant can carry a pile of leaves ten times its own weight. It chews the leaves to a pulp, which then decays. Strands of fungus grow on the pulp. The ants then eat this fungus. Carpenter ants get their name from their ability to make holes in wood for nesting.

A number of birds follow swarms of ants to eat larger insects and reptiles that are stirred from their hiding places by the thousands of moving ants.

MACAWS AND TOUCANS

Rainforests are teeming with birds that live in the two upper levels, the tallest branches and the canopy. Many, like the macaw and toucan, have developed special traits that help them live there.

Macaw

Macaws belong to the family of birds called *Psittaciformes*. They get this name from the pigment, psittacin, which gives them their brilliant colors. The 17 species of macaws are related to parrots and have a strong beak that curves down. The tip of their upper beak is sharp, to rip and tear with. Macaws eat fruit, seeds and nuts. The macaw has a long tail. However, it has fewer, stronger, feathers than most other birds. The hyacinth macaw, 39.4 inches (100 cm) in length, is the largest in the world. The smallest, the northeastern macaw of South America, is one-third that size.

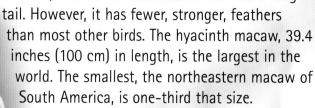

This is the rainbow colored macaw.

Social birds

Macaws are social birds and choose their partners early in life. If one dies, the other often does not live very much longer. Macaws nest in tree hollows. Macaws are noisy, intelligent birds that can imitate well. This makes them popular pets. This has led to several species, like the Spix's macaw, becoming extinct in the wild.

The macaw's feet have two toes in front and two at the back, which gives them a good grip.

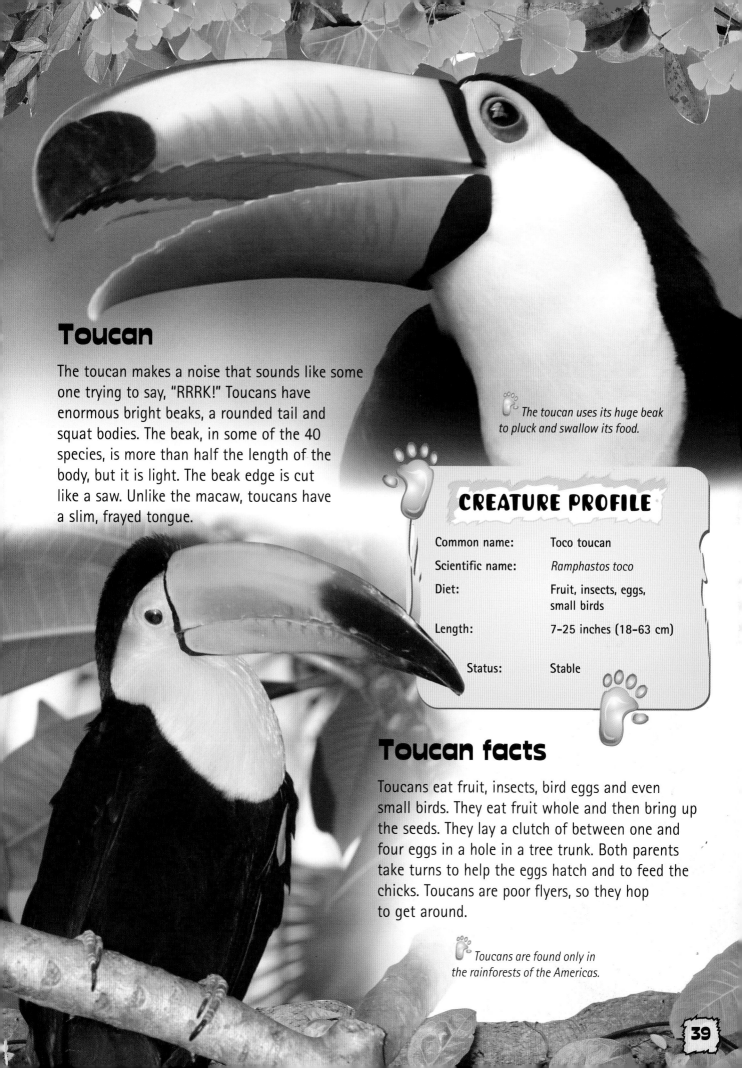

Toucan

The toucan makes a noise that sounds like some one trying to say, "RRRK!" Toucans have enormous bright beaks, a rounded tail and squat bodies. The beak, in some of the 40 species, is more than half the length of the body, but it is light. The beak edge is cut like a saw. Unlike the macaw, toucans have a slim, frayed tongue.

The toucan uses its huge beak to pluck and swallow its food.

CREATURE PROFILE

Common name:	Toco toucan
Scientific name:	*Ramphastos toco*
Diet:	Fruit, insects, eggs, small birds
Length:	7-25 inches (18-63 cm)
Status:	Stable

Toucan facts

Toucans eat fruit, insects, bird eggs and even small birds. They eat fruit whole and then bring up the seeds. They lay a clutch of between one and four eggs in a hole in a tree trunk. Both parents take turns to help the eggs hatch and to feed the chicks. Toucans are poor flyers, so they hop to get around.

Toucans are found only in the rainforests of the Americas.

OTHER BIRDS

Rainforests are home to a large variety of birds. Some can fly well, others not so well. Some are completely flightless and hop to get around.

Cassowary

Cassowaries are flightless bird of Australia and New Guinea that run at 30 miles per hour (48 km/h). Cassowaries kick in self-defense with powerful legs that have three-toed feet with sharp claws. The middle claw is 5 inches (12 cm) long and can rip an enemy apart. Cassowaries have a bony crest on their head which they use to clear a path through the forest. Their feathers look like a shaggy wig. Cassowaries eat fruit, insects, frogs and even snakes.

The cassowary helps to disperse seeds through the rainforests.

Quetzal

The quetzal has a beautiful tail about 39 inches (1 m) long.

The quetzal is a large, colorful bird of South America. The male is about 14 inches (35 cm) in length and has a green tail 24 inches (61 cm) long. The quetzal lives alone and cannot fly well. This makes them an easy target for eagles and owls. It lays one or two blue eggs in the hole of a tree. Both parents incubate the eggs, which hatch in about two weeks. The male quetzal feeds its young if the mother is not around. The quetzal eats fruit, snails, frogs and insects.

Trogon

Trogons are found in most rainforests, especially in Central America and South America. They get their name from the Greek word for nibbling. These birds nibble away at trees to make a nesting hole. Their first and second toes face backward, unlike most other birds, whose first and fourth toes face the back. This makes their grip weak. Trogons have a short, broad bill. They eat fruit and insects and live mostly in trees.

This is a white tailed trogon.

CREATURE PROFILE

Common name:	Jabiru
Scientific name:	*Jabiru mycteria*
Length of bill:	11.8 inches (30 cm)
Height:	About 5 feet (1.5 m)
Wingspan:	8.5 feet (2.6 m)
Enemy:	Humans
Status:	Endangered

JABIRU

The jabiru stork is one of the largest birds. Its name means "swollen neck." It has a heavy bill that helps it catch frogs, snakes and even fish. It lives in large groups near the water, in marshes or near lagoons. The jabiru is found all the way from southern Mexico to northern Argentina. In November, this bird nests in tall trees along the marshy lowlands. By July, the young are ready to fly north with their parents.

The jabiru is the largest flying bird of the Americas.

RAINFORESTS IN DANGER

People have cut rainforests extensively to make homes for themselves.

Rainforests have existed for millions of years. Sadly, over the last few centuries, people have been cutting them down. Rainforests once made up 14 percent of Earth's land surface. Now they cover only 6 percent. Rainforests are home to thousands of plant and animal species. Experts say that the rainforests could be gone in less than 40 years.

We increase, animals decrease

About 1.5 acres (.6 ha) of rainforest are cleared every second to make room for the growing human population. The twentieth century saw more people born than ever before. In 1800, the population stood at about one billion, and by 1950, it was 2.6 billion. Today, it is 6.5 billion. While the human population grows, the animal population is dwindling fast because their homes are being cut down.

Animals are illegally hunted for various parts of their body, which are sold on the black market.

A matter of more

Rainforests are cut down because people need more space to live, more wood to build houses and make furniture with, and more land to grow crops on. Therefore, rainforest animals and birds lose their homes and die. Animals like tigers, pythons, monkeys and birds are killed for their skin, fur and feathers. Some people make jewelry out of animal teeth and claws. In some places, animal body parts are used for traditional medicine. Parrots, macaws and pythons are sold illegally as pets, and they seldom survive or have babies outside the rainforest.

Around the world

Cutting down forests, or deforestation, affects the whole world in more ways than we understand. If there are fewer trees to absorb greenhouse gases, like carbon dioxide and methane, the Earth becomes drier and hotter. This means the ice at the North Pole and the South Pole may start melting, causing rivers and seas to flood their banks. This will lead to large scale destruction of life and property. When forests are cut down, more soil flows away, or erodes, since rain falls directly onto the ground. Without trees there are no roots to keep the soil from being washed away. With fewer forests, there will also be less rain, which will in turn have a harmful effect on the climate of the Earth.

Floods will cause a lot of destruction, causing death of animals and humans, uprooting trees and destroying property.

Going, going, gone!

About 35 species become extinct every day in the world's tropical rainforests due to habitat loss and hunting. Already, several species of animals, insects and birds have been lost forever. For example, the golden frog vanished before scientists were able to collect any sample of this amphibian for study. Larger animals, like leopards and tigers, need larger spaces to stay healthy. When forests are cleared, the wild animals are forced to move to smaller habitats and often die. Migratory birds like the hummingbird, that only visit the rainforest once a year, will have nowhere to go in winter and may die. All life, even ours, is linked with the lives of animals and plants. If so many species of plants, animals, insects and birds become extinct, so may we!

The hummingbird may have no home to spend the cold winter season in and may therefore die.

Glossary

Ambush (AM-bush) To attack prey by surprise

Amphibian (am-FIH-bee-un) Animals that can live on land and in water

Amplify (AM-pluh-fy) To increase sound

Arboreal (ahr-BOR-ee-ul) Animals that live on trees

Boring (BOR-ing) Drilling a hole

Burrow (BUR-oh) To dig the soil

Cinchona (sing-KOH-nuh) A variety of tree that produces quinine, a medicine used to treat malaria

Constriction (kun-STRIK-shun) To squeeze to death

Disperse (dih-SPERS) To scatter

Extinction (ik-STINGK-shun) To exist no more

Frayed (FRAYD) Rough and worn out

Glance (GLANTS) To look or gaze at someone or something

Global warming (GLOH-bul WOR-ming) The heating up of the Earth's atmosphere

Leaf litter (LEEF LIH-ter) A pile of decayed leaves

Leaf stalk (LEEF STOK) A soft stem that connects the leaf to a branch or stem

Mammal (MA-mul) Warm-blooded animals, the females of which carry their babies inside their body and suckle their babies

Migratory (MY-gruh-tor-ee) Bird and animals that move from one place to another for better climactic conditions

Mythical (MITH-ih-kul) Not real

Nocturnal (nahk-TER-nul) Animals that are active at night

Glossary

Opposable thumb
(uh-POH-zuh-bul THUM)
Thumb of some animals that can be turned backwards to help in grasping objects

Periwinkle
(PER-ih-wing-kul) An evergreen shrub that yeilds medicines used for treating diabetes and even cancer

Pollinate (PAH-luh-nayt) To transfer pollen between plants for new growth

Predator (PREH-duh-ter) A creature that kills and eats the prey

Prehensile (pree-HENT-sul)
A tail that can grasp or grip

Primates (PRY-mayts)
Animals with good eyesight, flexible hands and feet and a large brain

Primitive (PRIH-muh-tiv)
Early stages of development

Proboscis (pruh-BAH-sus)
A long, tubelike organ in some insects that help to suck nectar

Regenerating
(rih-JEH-neh-rayt-ing) To grow again

Reticulated
(rih-TIH-kyuh-layt-ed)
Markings that form a network

Rosette (roh-ZET) Rings on the body of some animals, like jaguars

Scuttle (SKUH-tul) To move quickly

Shaggy (SHA-gee) Long, rough hai

Spur (SPUR) To move quickly

Squat (SKWAHT) Broad

Stalk (STOK) To follow prey

Tapir (TAY-pur) A large, nocturnal mammal

Terrestrial (teh-RES-tree-ul)
Animals that live on land

Vertebrate (VER-tuh-brut)
Animals with a backbone

Further Reading & Web Sites

Martin, James. *Boa Constrictors*. Mankato, MN: Capstone
  Press, 1995.

Martin, Patricia A. *Chimpanzees*. New York: Scholastic Library
  Publishing, 2002.

Swain, Gwenyth. *Tigers*. Minnetonka, MN: T&N Children's
  Publishing, 2002.

Thomson, Sarah L. *Amazing Tigers!*. New York: Wildlife Conservation
  Society, Harper Collins Publishers, 2005.

Due to the changing nature of Internet links, PowerKids Press has
developed an online list of Web sites related to the subject of this
book. This site is updated regularly. Please use this link to access
the list:
www.powerkidslinks.com/wcre/rain/

Index

Index